TOM MUNZ ARCHITEKT

Diese Buchreihe versammelt die Bauwerke einzelner, mit hohem Qualitätsanspruch ausgewählter jüngerer Schweizer Architekturschaffender. Seit 2004 kuratiere ich die Reihe *Anthologie* in der Form einfacher Werkdokumentationen. Sie ist vergleichbar mit der «Blütenlese», wie sie in der Literatur für eine Sammlung ausgewählter Texte angewendet wird. Es liegt in der Natur des Architektenberufs, dass die Erstlingswerke junger Architekturschaffender meist kleinere, übersichtliche Bauaufgaben sind. Sie sind eine Art Fingerübung, mit der sie das Erlernte anwenden und ihr architektonisches Sensorium erproben und entfalten können. Die Begabung und die Leidenschaft für das Metier lassen sich dabei früh in voller Deutlichkeit und Frische erkennen. So stecken in jedem der kleinen und grossen Projekte inspirierte Grundgedanken und Vorstellungen, die spielerisch und gleichermassen perfekt in architektonische Bilder, Formen und Räume umgesetzt werden. Damit wird mir wieder einmal bewusst, dass in der Architektur wie in anderen Kunstformen die Bilder und Ideen, die hinter dem Werk stehen, das Wesentliche sind. Es mag diese Intuition sein, die Kunstschaffende haben, und die dann über ihr Werk wie ein Funke auf die Betrachtenden überspringt, so wie es der italienische Philosoph Benedetto Croce in seinen Schriften eindringlich beschreibt.

Heinz Wirz
Verleger

This book series presents buildings by selected young Swiss architects that set themselves high quality standards. Since 2004, I have been curating the *Anthologie* series by simply documenting their oeuvre. The series can be compared to a literary anthology presenting a collection of selected texts. It is in the nature of the architectural profession that early works by young architects are mostly small, limited building tasks. They are a kind of five-finger exercise in which the architects apply what they have learnt, as well as testing and developing their architectural instincts. Talent and a passion for the profession can be seen at an early stage in all of its clarity and freshness. Each project, be it large or small, contains an inspired underlying concept and ideas that are playfully and consummately implemented as architectural images, forms and spaces. Thus, I am regularly reminded that in architecture, as in other art forms, the images and ideas behind the works are their essence. Perhaps this is the same intuition described so vividly by the Italian philosopher Benedetto Croce, one that is absorbed by the artist and flies like a spark via the work to the viewer.

Heinz Wirz
Publisher

TOM MUNZ ARCHITEKT

QUART

Werner Binotto
AUS DER REGION HERAUS

AUS DER REGION HERAUS

Werner Binotto

Die Ostschweiz ist eine Transitregion. Zwischen Voralpen und Bodensee gelegen, prägen internationale Strömungen das Land. Das zeigt sich auch und vor allem in der Baukultur. Äussere politische und wirtschaftliche Entwicklungen beeinflussten seit jeher die regionale Architektur. Sichtbar wird das in den Arbeiten «welscher» Baumeister, aber beispielsweise auch im Werk der Familie Grubenmann im 17. und 18. Jahrhundert. Vor dem Hintergrund einer eigenen profilierten Baukultur hat sie äussere Entwicklungen aufgenommen und adaptiert. Diese äusseren Einflüsse waren und sind Grundlage und Inspiration für Architekturschaffende.

Das Werk von Tom Munz steht in dieser Tradition. Seine Arbeiten sind elaborierte Ergebnisse der Auseinandersetzung mit tradierten Bauformen und zeitgenössischen Tendenzen. Die Entwürfe sind deshalb im Umgang mit dem Umfeld und bei der architektonischen Umsetzung unterschiedlich und vielschichtig. Sie befassen sich differenziert mit dem Ort und generieren daraus strategische Konzepte. Die Ergebnisse sind jedoch keinem Muster verpflichtet. Vielmehr gehen unterschiedliche Architekturformen und -sprachen nebeneinander her. So gibt es den spätmodernen, gut durchgearbeiteten Schweizer Sichtbetonbau ebenso wie das Wohnhaus Holzenstein in Romanshorn, das sorgsam eingefügte Nebengebäude Wohnhaus Dorfstrasse in Thal oder den konstruktiv informellen Schulungsbau im Botanischen Garten St. Gallen. Architektonisch unterschiedlich umgesetzt, ist ihnen eine sorgfältige, differenzierte Gestaltung der Volumen und eine detaillierte Ausführung gemeinsam. Hinter den Arbeiten stehen Erfahrung und Wissen, die in der Beschäftigung mit dem Bauhandwerk erarbeitet wurden.

Der Umgang mit dem sozialen Umfeld, der Dialog mit der Bauherrschaft, der schon bei den «Grubenmännern» massgeblich war, beeinflusst das Ergebnis ausserdem. Er ist, wie das Bauen als Lernprozess, Teil dieser regionalen Baukultur. Tom Munz sucht diese Auseinandersetzung. Allein der «Schöne Entwurf» genügt ihm nicht. Die Menschen wollen das Resultat verstehen, die Architekturschaffenden sind daher Teil der architektonischen Vermittlung. Auch diese Funktion zu erfüllen gelingt Tom Munz nachhaltig gut.

Werner Binotto

Eastern Switzerland is a transit region. Situated between the Alpine foothills and Lake Constance, international influences define the region. This is especially visible in its building culture. External political and economic developments have always had an effect on regional architecture, as the work of master builders in Romandy demonstrate. The same also applies to buildings by the Grubenmann family dating back to the 17th and 18th centuries. Against the backdrop of a very specific, high-profile building culture, they adopted and adapted external developments. Such external influences remain both an underlying principle and an inspiration.

The work of Tom Munz is part of that tradition. His designs are the elaborated results of an engagement with traditional building forms and contemporary trends. The designs are therefore varied and diverse due to his handling of the environment and the architectural implementation. They engage in detail with the location, using it to generate a strategic concept for the design. However, the results are not dedicated to a specific pattern. Instead, various architectural forms and languages stand side by side. Thus we see the late-Modern, well worked Swiss exposed concrete, such as the Holzenstein residential building in Romanshorn, or the carefully inserted auxiliary building for the Dorfstrasse house in Thal, as well as the structurally informal training building for the St. Gallen Botanic Garden. Architecturally implemented in contrasting ways, their common aspects are the volumes' careful, differentiated design and a detailed finish. The works are a testimony of the experience and knowledge developed by engaging with the craft of building.

Like the Grubenmann family in the past, the approach to the social environment and dialogue with the client further influence the result. Combined with a belief in building as a learning process, it forms part of regional building culture. Tom Munz seeks such engagement. A "beautiful design" alone is not enough. People want to grasp the result. Architects therefore play a communicating role, which Tom Munz manages sustainably.

«GRÜNER PAVILLON», BOTANISCHER GARTEN ST. GALLEN
2017–2020, Projektwettbewerb, 1. Rang

Winden- und Rankenpflanzen an Drahtseilen hüllen den Pavillon in ein lebendiges Pflanzenkleid. Eine Konstruktion aus regionalem Fichtenholz bildet das Gerüst des «Grünen Pavillons». Der Boden besteht aus einer versiegelten und geschliffenen Betonplatte, welche die Sonnenwärme speichert und in der Nacht langsam abgibt. Die über die Diagonale an der West- und Ostfassade angeordneten, raumhohen Lüftungsflügel sorgen für Durchlüftung und Kühlung. Die Deckenleuchter sind eine Spezialanfertigung aus der Ostschweiz. Der Kubus aus Wandschränken zoniert den offenen Raum in Eingangs-, Haupt- und Abstellraum. Vorhänge variieren die Durchlässigkeit der Fassade und organisieren die multifunktionalen Nutzungen als Schulungsraum, Vortragssaal, Eventlokalität, Arbeitsplatz und Lager.

"GREEN PAVILION", BOTANIC GARDEN, ST. GALLEN
2017–2020, project competition, 1st Place

Bindweeds and creepers on wires envelop the pavilion with a vibrant garb of green. A load-bearing structure made of regional spruce forms the framework of the "Green Pavilion". The floor consists of a sealed, polished concrete plate that stores the solar warmth and slowly releases the energy at night. The room-high ventilation wings are arranged over the diagonal between the west and east façades to provide fresh air and cooling. The ceiling lights were specially produced in Eastern Switzerland. The cube of wall-mounted cupboards zones the open space to create an entrance area, a main space and a storage room. Curtains vary the façade's permeability and organise the multifunctional uses to provide a training room, a lecture theatre, an event location, a workplace and a warehouse.

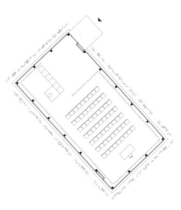

WOHNHAUS HOLZENSTEIN, ROMANSHORN
2017–2021, selektiver Studienauftrag, 1. Rang

Das Wohnhaus liegt in zweiter Baureihe eines Strassenzuges im Ortsbild-schutzgebiet. Westlich grenzt es an die Landwirtschaftszone mit freiem Blick auf den Bodensee. Der Baukörper verknüpft sich raumgreifend mit der Land-schaft und der bestehenden Umgebungsbebauung. Sein Ausdruck oszilliert zwischen Massivbau und Pavillon-Architektur. Damit reagiert der Entwurf auf die luftige Weite des Ortes mit dem See und die historische Struktur entlang der Holzensteinerstrasse. Im Grundriss arbeitet das Haus in seiner inneren Schichtung mit der historischen Typologie des Langhauses. Mit dem Nebenbau werden Hofräume geschaffen, welche die bäuerliche Zonierung im Freiraum interpretieren und die bestehende Massstäblichkeit aufnehmen.

HOLZENSTEIN RESIDENTIAL BUILDING, ROMANSHORN
2017–2021, selective contracted study, 1ˢᵗ Place

The construction site in the second development row of a street is situ-ated in a heritage preservation area, with an adjacent agricultural zone to the west, affording an open view of Lake Constance. The building is spatially interwoven with the landscape and the existing neighbourhood developments. Its expression oscillates between a solid structure and pa-vilion architecture, thereby reflecting the airy openness of the location with the lake and the historical structure along Holzensteinerstrasse. The building's floor plan develops its inner layers as an example of the his-torical typology of a longhouse. The auxiliary building provides courtyard spaces, interpreting the farming zones in the open space and adopting the existing scale.

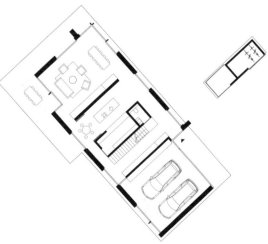

ERGÄNZUNGSBAU PRIMARSCHULE, FRASNACHT
2019–2021, selektiver Studienauftrag, 1. Rang

Der Ergänzungsbau des Schulareals ist in drei Bereiche gegliedert: Der erste Bereich, angefügt an die Turnhalle, organisiert die Funktionsräume. Angrenzend liegt die Erschliessungszone mit sämtlichen Verkehrsstrukturen. Im äusseren Bereich nach Süden sind alle Nutzräume angeordnet. Die hoch flexible Gestaltung der inneren Struktur hält den Nutzungsänderungen der nächsten Jahrzehnte stand. Die neu gestaltete Freianlage orientiert sich in ihrer Formensprache an der klaren Architektur der Neubauten. Deren präzise Setzung stärkt die räumliche Fassung der Pausenflächen. Der zentrale Pausenhof erhält eine grosszügige Überdachung. Als Verbindungsglied ist das Dach einerseits Wetterschutz, andererseits schafft es einen Ankunftsort und verleiht dem Schulhaus eine sichtbare Adresse und Identität.

PRIMARY SCHOOL EXTENSION, FRASNACHT
2019–2021, selective contracted study, 1st Place

The school extension building is structured in three sections: the first is connected to the sports hall and organises the functional rooms. The adjoining access zone contains all the mobility routes. All auxiliary rooms are arranged in the external area to the south. The maximum-flexibility design of the interior structure will cope with changes of use in the coming years. The newly designed open space is orientated towards the formal language of the neighbouring buildings' clear architecture. Their precise placement strengthens the spatial framing of the playground areas. The central playground enjoys a generous cover. This connecting element provides both protection from inclement weather and also an arrival space, giving the school a visible address and identity.

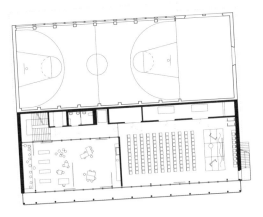

WOHNANLAGE WOHNEN AM BODENSEE, SCHWEIZ
2018–2022, Direktauftrag

Die Baukörper dieser Wohnanlage am Ufer des Bodensees gruppieren sich um eine hundertjährige Blutbuche. Die Publikation *Das Englische Haus* (1904/1905) von Hermann Muthesius und ein Wohnhaus von Bailey Scott in der Schweiz, das im Besitz der Bauherrschaft ist, waren ausschlaggebend für die Gestaltung dieses Werkes. Drei Hochbauten unterschiedlicher Massstäblichkeit bilden eine räumliche Einheit und schaffen mittels Stellung und Durchbildung eine differenzierte Abfolge von Hof- und Aussenräumen. Auf die Tiefe des Bodensees reagiert der Entwurf mit einer akzentuierten Höhenstaffelung der eingeschossigen Bauten, welche die innere räumliche Organisation im Ausdruck vereint. Prägend sind die handgeformten Vollziegel, die mit den Mauerabschlüssen aus Ortbeton eine gewebte Tektonik schaffen.

HOUSING BY LAKE CONSTANCE, SWITZERLAND
2018–2022, direct contract

The housing development on the shore of Lake Constance is grouped around a hundred-year-old copper beech. "The English House" by Hermann Muthesius and a residential building by Bailey Scott in Switzerland, which is owned by the client, formed the basis of the common language for this project. Three buildings with different scales form a unity, achieving a differentiated series of courtyard and exterior spaces through their placement and development. The design reacts to the horizontal layering at Lake Constance through the accentuated staggering of heights for the single-storey buildings, thereby also unifying the internal spatial organisation through their expression. The hand-crafted solid bricks define the appearance, combining with the wall conclusions made of in-situ cast concrete to create textile tectonics.

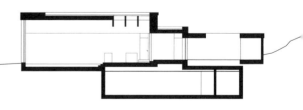

WOHNHAUS DORFSTRASSE, THAL
2017–2018, Direktauftrag

Rund um das denkmalgeschützte Bürgerhaus haben sich während der letzten 150 Jahre etliche Nutzungserweiterungen vollzogen. Die Rückbauten und die sanfte Sanierung des Gebäudes machen die Grundidee des hofartigen Gefüges und die Qualitäten des historisch geprägten Ortes wieder erlebbar. Aussen und Innen sind konsequent als Einheit entworfen. Die Raumskulptur aus Beton spannt sich – aussen dunkel, innen hell – wie eine schützende Hülle durch das gesamte Haus. Die als Holzelementbau gefertigte Fassade wurde mit regionalen Handwerksleuten erarbeitet. Die mit Öl bemalten und mit dunklen Pigmenten verbrannten Holzlatten kleiden den Baukörper in eine sattschwarze Hülle. Die gebeizten Dreischichtplatten überführen das optische und haptische Konzept partiell ins Innere.

RESIDENTIAL BUILDING, DORFSTRASSE, THAL
2017–2018, direct contract

Over the last 150 years, numerous use extensions have developed all around the preservation-listed municipal building. Measures to dismantle these and gently refurbish the building make the underlying idea of the courtyard structure and the inherent qualities of the historical location perceptible again. Both the exterior and interior are conceived as a consistent unit. Outwards dark and inwardly light, the spatial sculpture of concrete is spanned like a protective envelope over the entire building. The façade consisting of wooden elements was developed together with regional artisans. The flamed wooden slats, which were treated with an oil containing dark pigments, clad the building in a rich black shell. The stained, three-ply boards partially transfer the visual and tactile idea to the interior.

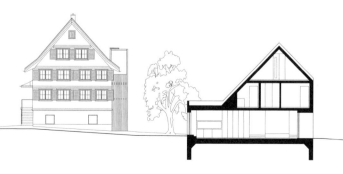

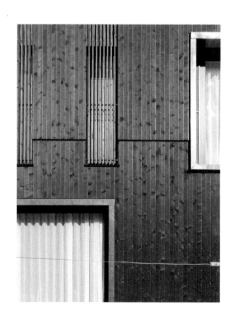

WOHNHAUS STERNENSTRASSE, UZWIL
2015–2017, Direktauftrag

Das Quartier, in dem der Bauort liegt, hat sich in den letzten Jahren vom Industrie- und Gewerbegebiet zu einem Wohnquartier gewandelt. Das leicht abfallende Grundstück grenzt an seiner westlichen Schmalseite an den aufgeschütteten Bahndamm aus dem 19. Jahrhundert. Das Konzept geht unprätentiös auf den ortsbaulichen Kontext ein. Durch die Setzung, Massstäblichkeit und die räumlichen Bezüge soll die ursprüngliche Nutzung erlebbar bleiben. Die progressive Wohnform sucht die atmosphärische Unmittelbarkeit eines Industriebaus. Der lang gezogene orthogonale Baukörper entwickelt sich parallel zur südlichen Parzellengrenze. In seinen drei Geschossen sind 14 Wohneinheiten entstanden. Der Vierspänner erschliesst alle Wohnungen über ein Treppenhaus an der Nordfassade.

RESIDENTIAL BUILDING, STERNENSTRASSE, UZWIL
2015–2017, direct contract

In recent years, the building site's surroundings have transformed from an industrial and commercial area to a residential neighbourhood. The gently sloping property borders with the 19th-century railway embankment on its narrow, western side. The concept is unpretentiously developed out of the local context. Its placement, scale and spatial references are aimed at making the original use perceptible. The progressive residential form is atmospherically inspired by the directness of industrial structures. The elongated, orthogonal volume develops parallel to the southern boundary of the plot. 14 housing units were created in the three-storey building. The four-winged volume connects all apartments via a staircase at its north façade.

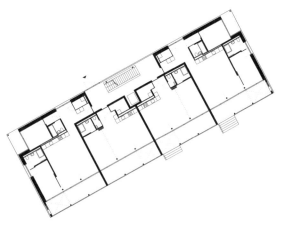

WOHNHAUS SCHLOSSGASSE, WEINFELDEN
2020–2022, Direktauftrag

Der Bauort liegt am einst weinbäuerlich geprägten Südhang des Ottenbergs. Die historische Prägung nimmt das Wohnhaus in sich auf. Ein zur Strasse traufständiger zweigeschossiger Baukörper bildet einen Strassenplatz. Der Hauptfirst verläuft quer dazu nach Westen und bildet so einen Hofraum mit einem unverbaubaren Blick auf die Stadt und das Umland. Als Bezugsgrösse diente die historische Typologie der bestehenden Hofbauten am Hang. Der Holzbau zeigt sich aussen in einem Kleid aus sägerauem Holz und innen in einer geölten Holzschalung. Die feinen Höhenstaffelungen im Erdgeschoss und die Überhöhe im Wohnbereich schaffen räumliche Beziehungen, die das Familienleben über die Geschosse hinweg vereint.

RESIDENTIAL BUILDING, SCHLOSSGASSE, WEINFELDEN
2020–2022, direct contract

The building site is situated on the south-facing slope of the Ottenberg, which was once a vineyard. The residential building picks up on this historical character. The two-storey volume, its eaves side facing the street, creates a street square. The main roof ridge runs perpendicular to that line, towards the west, forming a courtyard area with a view of the town and countryside that cannot be obscured by further development. The historical typography of the existing courtyard buildings on the slope served as a reference. The wooden volume presents its exterior in an envelope of rough-sawn wood, while its interior consists of oiled wooden cladding. The finely staggered heights on the ground floor and the extra-high living areas create spatial references that unify family life on the different levels.

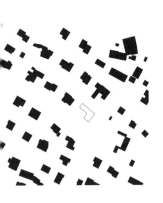

ERSATZNEUBAU AUSSEGNUNGSHALLE, OBERRIET

2014–2016, eingeladener Projektwettbewerb, 1. Rang

Die Baufläche für die neue Aussegnungshalle war durch bestehende Grab- und Urnenfelder eingeschränkt und verlangte nach einer Interpretation dieses Sakraltypus und einer angemessenen Raumatmosphäre. Die neue Setzung in der südwestlichen Parzellenecke stärkt die räumliche Beziehung zur Kapelle. Die Zahl Drei und ihre Potenzierung bildet den Kern des konzeptionellen Ansatzes. Die vertikale und horizontale Durchbildung des Baukörpers aus jeweils drei Elementen setzt sich auch in der Materialisierung fort. Sockel und Dach als Verbindungselemente zwischen Himmel und Erde sind in schalungsglattem Beton ausgeführt. Dazwischen spannen sich Fassaden aus gestocktem Beton auf. Die Räume bilden ein komplementäres Gegengewicht zum äusseren Erscheinungsbild.

REPLACEMENT BUILDING, FUNERAL PARLOUR, OBERRIET

2014–2016, invitation project competition, 1st Place

The perimeter of the new funeral parlour was surrounded by grounds with graves and urnfields, requiring an appropriate spatial atmosphere in accordance with the religious interpretation. The building's new placement in the southwestern corner of the plot strengthens the spatial relationship to the chapel. The number three and its factors form the conceptual approach. The vertical and horizontal structure of the volume in three respective elements is also reflected in the materialisation. The base and roof, connecting elements between heaven and earth, are conceived in smoothly formworked concrete. The façades are made of bush-hammered concrete, while the rooms create a dialectic contrast to the outdoor experience.

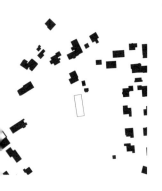

WERKVERZEICHNIS
Auswahl Bauten, Projekte und Wettbewerbe

2015		Selektiver Studienauftrag Gemeindesaal Moulen (2. Rang)
	1	Ersatzneubau Wohnhaus A, Egnach
2016		Ersatzneubau Aussegnungshalle, Oberriet (eingeladener Projektwettbewerb 2014, 1. Rang) Selektiver Studienauftrag Erweiterung Forster Rohner AG, St. Gallen
2017		Selektiver Studienauftrag Neubau Turnhalle, Wilen Offener Projektwettbewerb Schulhaus Wiesenau, St. Margrethen (letzter Rundgang) Selektiver Studienauftrag Wohnanlage Wohnen im Waldacker, St. Gallen Umbau Wohnhaus Z, Speicherschwendi, Speicher Wohnhaus Sternenstrasse, Uzwil
	2	Wohnhaus A, Niederhelfenschwil

1

2018		Eingeladener Studienauftrag Passerelle Oberstockenweg, St. Gallen (2. Rang) Selektiver Studienauftrag Städtebauliches Konzept Werkraum, Wattwil (2. Rang) Wohnhaus Dorfstrasse, Thal
	3	Cigar Lounge Hotel Uzwil, Uzwil Sanierung Hotel Uzwil, Uzwil
	4	Raiffeisenbank Obertoggenburg, Nesslau (selektiver Studienauftrag 2015, 1. Rang) Umbau Eggel & Partner AG, St. Gallen

2

2019		Offener Projektwettbewerb Neugestaltung Marktplatz Bohl, St. Gallen (2. Rang) Umbau Wohnhaus K, St. Gallen
2020	5	Selektiver Studienauftrag Erweiterung Schulgemeinde Niederwil
	6	Umbau Raiffeisenbank, Balgach «Grüner Pavillon», Botanischer Garten St. Gallen (Projektwettbewerb, 2017, 1. Rang)

| 2021 | | Ergänzungsbau Primarschule, Frasnacht (selektiver Studienauftrag 2019, 1. Rang) Wohnhaus Holzenstein, Romanshorn (selektiver Studienauftrag 2017, 1. Rang) Sanierung Technopark, Zürich (selektiver Studienauftrag 2015, 1. Rang) |

3

2022	7	Eingeladener Studienauftrag OST, St. Gallen (2. Rang)
	8	Selektiver Projektwettbewerb FLAWA-Areal, Flawil (2. Rang) Wohnhaus Schlossgasse, Weinfelden Wohnhaus Höhenweg, St. Gallen Wohnanlage Wohnen am Bodensee, Schweiz
	9	Wohnanlage Am Landberg, Flawil

4

5

6

7

LIST OF WORKS
Selection of buildings, projects and competitions

2015		Selective study contract, Moulen Community Hall (2ⁿᵈ Place)
	1	Replacement residential building A, Egnach
2016		Replacement building, funeral parlour, Oberriet (invitation project competition in 2014, 1ˢᵗ Place)
		Selective contracted study, extension, Forster Rohner AG, St. Gallen
2017		Selective contracted study, new building, sports hall, Wilen
		Open project competition, Wiesenau school building, St. Margrethen (final round)
		Selective contracted study, Wohnen im Waldacker housing estate, St. Gallen
		Conversion, House Z, residential building, Speicherschwendi, Speicher
		Residential building, Sternenstrasse, Uzwil
	2	House A, residential building, Niederhelfenschwil
2018		Invitation contracted study, Passerelle Oberstockenweg, St. Gallen (2ⁿᵈ Place)
		Selective contracted study, Werkraum urban-planning concept, Wattwil (2ⁿᵈ Place)
		Residential building, Dorfstrasse, Thal
	3	Cigar Lounge, Hotel Uzwil, Uzwil
		Refurbishment, Hotel Uzwil, Uzwil
	4	Raiffeisenbank Obertoggenburg, Nesslau (selective contracted study in 2015, 1ˢᵗ Place)
		Conversion, Eggel & Partner AG, St. Gallen
2019		Open project competition, redesign, Marktplatz Bohl, St. Gallen (2ⁿᵈ Place)
		Conversion, House Wohnhaus K, residential building, St. Gallen
2020	5	Selective contracted study, school extension, Niederwil
	6	Conversion, Raiffeisenbank, Balgach
		"Green Pavilion", Botanic Garden, St. Gallen (project competition in 2017, 1ˢᵗ Place)
2021		Primary school extension, Frasnacht (selective contracted study in 2019, 1ˢᵗ Place)
		Holzenstein residential building, Romanshorn (selective contracted study in 2017, 1ˢᵗ Place)
		Technopark refurbishment, Zurich (selective contracted study in 2015, 1ˢᵗ Place)
2022	7	Invitation contracted study, OST, St. Gallen (2ⁿᵈ Place)
	8	Selective project competition, FLAWA-Areal, Flawil (2ⁿᵈ Place)
		Residential building, Schlossgasse, Weinfelden
		Residential building, Höhenweg, St. Gallen
		Housing by Lake Constance, Switzerland
	9	Am Landberg housing estate, Flawil

8

9

10

11

12

13

14

15

16

TOM MUNZ

1976	Geboren in Wil
1992–1997	Ausbildung zum Hochbauzeichner bei Architekt Alex Künzle, Flawil
2000–2004	Architekturstudium an der Hochschule für Angewandte Wissenschaften, St. Gallen
2005–2007	Architekturstudium bei Prof. Hans Kollhoff an der ETH, Zürich
2005–2009	Mitarbeit bei Binotto & Gähler Architekten, St. Gallen
2008–2012	Vorstandsmitglied Thurgauer Heimatschutz
2009–2013	Partner bei fingermunz architekten, St. Gallen
2013–	Selbstständiger Architekt
2015–2017	Mitglied der Redaktionskommission *archithese*
2017–2020	Dozent an der Hochschule für Angewandte Wissenschaften, St. Gallen

MITARBEITENDE

Aline Kopp, Eva Schulthess, Matthias Ulmann,
Deborah Weber, Sahra Khan, Tobias Finckh, Silja Munz,
Lia Taricco, Marcel Bruderer, Alicia Chanton,
Lukas Meier, Marc Andreas Lindenmeyer,
Stefanie Geser, Lucia Mandura, Cédric Ruppanner,
Benjamin Maeder, Friedrich Kühnemund, Miriam Gohm,
Nina Heeb, Thomas Jochum

AUSZEICHNUNGEN

2004	*Swiss Engineering Award:* Beste Diplomarbeit an der Hochschule für Angewandte Wissenschaften, St. Gallen
2015	Shortlist Baunetz 2016: Ersatzneubau Wohnhaus A, Egnach
2016	*Timber House of the World:* Ersatzneubau Wohnhaus A, Egnach
	Building of the Year 2016 (Nominierung): Ersatzneubau Wohnhaus A, Egnach
2019	*Die schönsten Restaurants und Bars in Europa 2019:* Cigar Lounge Hotel Uzwil, Uzwil

TOM MUNZ

1976	Born in Wil
1992–1997	Apprenticeship as a draughtsman under the architect Alex Künzle, Flawil
2000–2004	Studied Architecture at FHS St. Gallen
2005–2007	Studied Architecture under Prof. Hans Kollhoff, ETH Zurich
2005–2009	Employed at Binotto & Gähler Architekten, St. Gallen
2008–2012	Committee Member, Swiss Heritage Society, Thurgau Section
2009–2013	Partner, fingermunz architekten, St. Gallen
2013–	Freelance architect
2015–2017	Editorial Board Member, *archithese*
2017–2020	Lecturer, FHS St. Gallen

TEAM

Aline Kopp, Eva Schulthess, Matthias Ulmann,
Deborah Weber, Sahra Khan, Tobias Finckh,
Silja Munz, Lia Taricco, Marcel Bruderer, Alicia Chanton,
Lukas Meier, Marc Andreas Lindenmeyer,
Stefanie Geser, Lucia Mandura, Cédric Ruppanner,
Benjamin Maeder, Friedrich Kühnemund,
Miriam Gohm, Nina Heeb, Thomas Jochum

AWARDS

2004	*Swiss Engineering Award:* Best Graduation Paper, FHS St. Gallen
2015	Shortlist, Baunetz 2016: Replacement residential building A, Egnach
2016	*Timber House of the World:* Replacement residential building A, Egnach
	Building of the Year 2016 (nominated): Replacement residential building A, Egnach
2019	*Die schönsten Restaurants und Bars in Europa 2019:* Cigar Lounge, Hotel Uzwil, Uzwil

BIBLIOGRAFIE (Auswahl)

2016   «Der demonstrative Verzicht» [Ersatzneubau
              Wohnhaus A, Egnach], in: Thomas Walliser, *Modulor*
              5/2016, Urdorf, S. 76–80
              «less is more» [Ersatzneubau Wohnhaus A, Egnach], in:
              Katharina Matzig / Wolfgang Bachmann, *Grundrissatlas*
              Einfamilienhaus, München, S. 196–199
              «Kleines Frankreich am Bodensee» [Ersatzneubau
              Wohnhaus A, Egnach], in: Sandra Depner, *FIRST*,
              Fachmagazin Holzbau Schweiz 2/2016, Zürich, S. 38–43
2017   «Architektur des Abschieds» [Ersatzneubau
              Aussegnungshalle Oberriet], in: Joshua Loher / Sarah
              Peter Vogt, *Bauen im Rheintal*, Zürich, S. 50–51
              «Ersatzneubau» [Ersatzneubau Wohnhaus A, Egnach],
              in: Katrin Bühler / Julia Heinemann, *Living in Wood*,
              Salenstein, S. 214–217
2018   Carmen Nagel Eschrich, «Ein Haus mit Hof»
              [Wohnhaus A, Niederhelfenschwil], in:
              Das Einfamilienhaus, 2/2018, S. 46–54
              Swiss-Architects.com, «Industrielle Wohnwelten»
              [Wohnhaus Sternenstrasse, Uzwil], in: *SonntagsZeitung*,
              2. Dezember 2018
              Hubertus Adam, «Am Übergang» [Ersatzneubau
              Aussegnungshalle Oberriet], in: *db deutsche bauzeitung*
              «Architektur der Stille», 11/2018, S. 18–23
2019   Verena Kaup [Cigar Lounge Hotel Uzwil, Uzwil], in: *Die*
              schönsten Restaurants & Bars, München, S. 162–165
2020   «Mehrfamilienhaus Sternenstrasse» [Wohnhaus
              Sternenstrasse, Uzwil], in: Sabrina Terwolbeck,
              Wohnen. Zukunftsorientiertes Bauen, Münster,
              S. 226–231
              Chris van Uffelen, «Wohnen im Dorf» [Wohnhaus
              Dorfstrasse, Thal], in: *Architektenhäuser in der Schweiz &*
              Österreich, Salenstein, S. 266–269
2021   Dennis Krause, «Neubau Wohnhaus F» [Wohnhaus
              Holzenstein, Romanshorn], in: *Jahrbuch der Architektur*
              20/21, Münster, S. 278–283

WERNER BINOTTO (Textbeitrag)

1973–1976   Lehre als Bauzeichner
1979–1986   Studium der Architektur an Akademien in Düsseldorf
              und Wien
1986–2006   Freischaffender Architekt
2006–2020   Kantonsbaumeister des Kantons St. Gallen
              Lebt und arbeitet in der Ostschweiz

BIBLIOGRAPHY (selection)

2016	"Der demonstrative Verzicht" [replacement building A, Egnach]. In: Thomas Walliser: *Modulor* 5/2016, Urdorf, p. 76–80 "less is more" [replacement building A, Egnach]. In: Katharina Matzig / Wolfgang Bachmann: *Grundrissatlas Einfamilienhaus*, Munich, p. 196–199 "Kleines Frankreich am Bodensee" [replacement building A, Egnach]. In: Sandra Depner: *FIRST, Fachmagazin Holzbau Schweiz* 2/2016, Zurich, p. 38–43
2017	"Architektur des Abschieds" [replacement building, funeral parlour, Oberriet]. In: Joshua Loher / Sarah Peter Vogt: *Bauen im Rheintal*, Zurich, p. 50–51 "Ersatzneubau" [replacement building A, Egnach]. In: Katrin Bühler / Julia Heinemann: *Living in Wood*, Salenstein, p. 214–217
2018	Carmen Nagel Eschrich: "Ein Haus mit Hof" [residential building A, Niederhelfenschwil]. In: *Das Einfamilienhaus*, 2/2018, p. 46–54 Swiss-Architects.com: "Industrielle Wohnwelten" [residential building in Sternenstrasse, Uzwil]. In: *SonntagsZeitung*, December 2, 2018 Hubertus Adam: "Am Übergang" [replacement building, funeral parlour, Oberriet]. In: *db deutsche bauzeitung "Architektur der Stille"*, 11/2018, p. 18–23
2019	Verena Kaup [Cigar Lounge, Hotel Uzwil, Uzwil]. In: *Die schönsten Restaurants & Bars*, Munich, p. 162–165
2020	"Mehrfamilienhaus Sternenstrasse" [residential building, Sternenstrasse, Uzwil]. In: Sabrina Terwolbeck, *Wohnen. Zukunftsorientiertes Bauen*, Münster, p. 226–231 Chris van Uffelen: "Wohnen im Dorf" [residential building, Dorfstrasse, Thal]. In: *Architektenhäuser in der Schweiz & Österreich*, Salenstein, p. 266–269
2021	Dennis Krause: "Neubau Wohnhaus F" [Holzenstein residential building, Romanshorn]. In: *Jahrbuch der Architektur* 20/21, Münster, p. 278–283

WERNER BINOTTO (article)

1973–1976	Apprenticeship as a draughtsman
1979–1986	Studied Architecture at the Academies in Düsseldorf and Vienna
1986–2006	Freelance architect
2006–2020	Cantonal Master Builder, Canton of St. Gallen Lives and works in Eastern Switzerland

ARCHITEKTUR, ZUM GEFÜHL ERHOBENE KONSTRUKTION
Frei nach Karl Friedrich Schinkel

ARCHITECTURE, CONSTRUCTION ELEVATED TO FEELING
Freely adapted from Karl Friedrich Schinkel

Vgl. Goerd Peschken, *Das Architektonische Lehrbuch von Karl Friedrich Schinkel*, München 2001, S. 50.

See Goerd Peschken: *Das Architektonische Lehrbuch von Karl Friedrich Schinkel*, Munich 2001, p. 50.

Finanzielle und ideelle Unterstützung

Ein besonderer Dank gilt den Institutionen und Sponsorfirmen, deren finanzielle Unterstützungen wesentlich zum Entstehen dieser Buchreihe beitragen. Ihr kulturelles Engagement ermöglicht ein fruchtbares und freundschaftliches Zusammenwirken von Baukultur und Bauwirtschaft.

Financial and conceptual support

Special thanks to our sponsors and institutions whose financial support has helped us so much with the production of this series of books. Their cultural commitment is a valuable contribution to fruitful and cordial collaboration between the culture and economics of architecture.

Thurgau
Lotteriefonds

Walo Bertschinger AG
Ostschweiz, Goldach

real.stein

Real Stein AG, Gibswil ZH

Stutz

STUTZ AG Bauunternehmung,
Hefenhofen

zomo**form** ⊪⊪⊪⊪

Zomo form AG, Au SG

EGGEL & PARTNER
Baumanagement

Eggel & Partner AG, St. Gallen

 **Blumer**
Lehmann
Holzbau | Engineering

Blumer-Lehmann AG,
Gossau

Tom Munz Architekt
48. Band der Reihe *Anthologie*
Herausgeber: Heinz Wirz, Luzern
Konzept: Heinz Wirz; Tom Munz Architekt, St. Gallen
Projektleitung: Quart Verlag, Linus Wirz
Textbeitrag: Werner Binotto, Altstätten
Objekttexte: Tom Munz Architekt
Textlektorat deutsch: Dr. Britta Schröder, schroeder-works.de, Friedberg
Textlektorat englisch: Benjamin Liebelt, Berlin
Übersetzung deutsch – englisch: Benjamin Liebelt, Berlin
Fotos: Ladina Bischof, Arbon, S. 9–19, 29–35, 43–53, 58–59, 60–61 (Nr. 3, 6);
Jürg Zürcher, St. Gallen, S. 21–27, 60 (Nr. 4); Joshua Loher, Widnau, S. 37–41,
55–57, 69; Katia Rudnicki, St. Gallen, S. 60 (Nr. 1, 2); Elisa Florian, St. Gallen,
S. 62 (Nr. 9)
Renderings: Tom Munz Architekt, St. Gallen, S. 60–63 (Nr. 5, 7, 8, 10, 11, 12, 13,
14, 15, 16)
Redesign: BKVK, Basel – Beat Keusch, Angelina Köpplin-Stützle
Grafische Umsetzung: Quart Verlag Luzern
Lithos: Printeria, Luzern
Druck: DZA Druckerei zu Altenburg GmbH

Tom Munz Architekt
Volume 48 of the series *Anthologie*
Edited by: Heinz Wirz, Lucerne
Concept: Heinz Wirz; Tom Munz Architekt, St. Gallen
Project management: Quart Verlag, Linus Wirz
Article by: Werner Binotto, Altstätten
Project descriptions: Tom Munz Architekt
German text editing: Dr. Britta Schröder, schroeder-works.de, Friedberg
English text editing: Benjamin Liebelt, Berlin
German – English translation: Benjamin Liebelt, Berlin
Photos: Ladina Bischof, Arbon, p. 9–19, 29–35, 43–53, 58–59, 60–61
(Nos. 3, 6); Jürg Zürcher, St. Gallen, p. 21–27, 60 (No. 4); Joshua Loher,
Widnau, p. 37–41, 55–57, 69; Katia Rudnicki, St. Gallen, p. 60 (Nos. 1, 2);
Elisa Florian, St. Gallen, p. 62 (No. 9)
Renderings: Tom Munz Architekt, St. Gallen, p. 60–63 (Nos. 5, 7, 8, 10, 11,
12, 13, 14, 15, 16)
Redesign: BKVK, Basel – Beat Keusch, Angelina Köpplin-Stützle
Graphic design: Quart Verlag Luzern
Lithos: Printeria, Lucerne
Printing: DZA Druckerei zu Altenburg GmbH

Der Quart Verlag wird vom Bundesamt für
Kultur für die Jahre 2021–2024 unterstützt.
Quart Publishers is being supported
by the Federal Office of Culture for the
years 2021–2024.

Quart Verlag GmbH
Denkmalstrasse 2, CH-6006 Luzern
books@quart.ch, www.quart.ch

Anthologie
Werkberichte junger Architekturschaffender

**Anthologie
Work reports on young architects**

*inserted booklet with translation